Gaming and eSports

LEVEL UP
SECRETS OF THE GAMES WE LOVE

Kaitlyn Duling

ROURKE'S SCHOOL to HOME CONNECTIONS
BEFORE AND DURING READING ACTIVITIES

Before Reading: *Building Background Knowledge and Vocabulary*

Building background knowledge can help children process new information and build upon what they already know. Before reading a book, it is important to tap into what children already know about the topic. This will help them develop their vocabulary and increase their reading comprehension.

Questions and Activities to Build Background Knowledge:

1. Look at the front cover of the book and read the title. What do you think this book will be about?
2. What do you already know about this topic?
3. Take a book walk and skim the pages. Look at the table of contents, photographs, captions, and bold words. Did these text features give you any information or predictions about what you will read in this book?

Vocabulary: *Vocabulary Is Key to Reading Comprehension*

Use the following directions to prompt a conversation about each word.

- Read the vocabulary words.
- What comes to mind when you see each word?
- What do you think each word means?

Vocabulary Words:
- cheat codes
- crossover
- developer
- exergames
- franchises
- modification
- sandbox

During Reading: *Reading for Meaning and Understanding*

To achieve deep comprehension of a book, children are encouraged to use close reading strategies. During reading, it is important to have children stop and make connections. These connections result in deeper analysis and understanding of a book.

 ### Close Reading a Text

During reading, have children stop and talk about the following:

- Any confusing parts
- Any unknown words
- Text to text, text to self, text to world connections
- The main idea in each chapter or heading

Encourage children to use context clues to determine the meaning of any unknown words. These strategies will help children learn to analyze the text more thoroughly as they read.

When you are finished reading this book, turn to the next-to-last page for **After-Reading Questions** and an **Activity**.

Table of Contents

Easter Eggs 4
All-Time Greats 6
Epic Battles 12
Rules of the Game 18
In the Sandbox 24
Memory Game 30
Index 31
After-Reading Questions 31
Activity 31
About the Author 32

EASTER EGGS

What's your favorite video game? How many times have you played it? For gamers who play their favorites over and over again, games can feel like a second home. But that doesn't mean they're boring! One fun part of gaming is discovering the secrets inside the games. The hidden surprises inside video games are called "Easter eggs." Just like real Easter eggs, they're fun to search for and collect. Ready to unlock some top-secret video game secrets? Let's go on an Easter egg hunt.

There is a human gene called Sonic Hedgehog! It helps shape the brain, eyes, and other parts of the body.

The world of *Minecraft* is about seven times larger than Earth.

Game Boy was the first video game console to be played in space.

There is a hiding spot in *Pac-Man* where the ghosts cannot find and eat the character.

In 1996, *Chex Quest* became the first video game to be offered as a cereal box prize. Today you can download it and play online.

ALL-TIME GREATS

New video games (and Easter eggs!) are created every day. There are hundreds of thousands, maybe even *millions* of games available. A few have stood the test of time. These classic video game **franchises** are beloved around the world. With dozens of games across multiple consoles, each of these franchises is packed with tricks, cheats, and secrets.

FRANCHISES (FRAN-chize-ez): a series of related works (such as video games) which include the same characters or different characters in the same fictional universe

SUPER SECRET MARIO

Remember the seven Koopaling characters from the *Super Mario* series? You might not know that their names come from famous musicians! Ludvig von Koopa = Ludwig von Beethoven; Iggy Koopa = Iggy Pop; Roy Koopa = Roy Orbison

MARIO
$30,250,000,000

POKEMON
$90,000,000,000

CALL OF DUTY
$17,000,000,000

THE TOP 3 BEST-SELLING VIDEO GAME FRANCHISES OF ALL TIME

Cheat codes may not be the most honest way to play through video games. But they can make the experience more fun. The "king of cheat codes" is the Konami Code. The secret code has appeared in many games for decades. Players can use it in *Overwatch*, *Contra*, *Viva Piñata*, and more. Just use your controller to enter "up, up, down, down, left, right, left, right, B, A." Watch the Disney film *Wreck-It Ralph* closely, and you'll see King Candy using the code to unlock a door!

ANCIENT EGG

The very first Easter egg in video game history appears in Starship 1. The 1977 Atari game features the secret message "Hi Ron!" and 10 extra lives for the player. The game's engineer, Ron Milner, exposed the secret in an online blog in 2017.

CHEAT CODES (cheet kodes): something (such as a button, password, or sequence) that activates a hidden feature or capability in a video game

Some Easter eggs have nothing to do with the game you're playing. They can be nods to other games and characters. One fun example: *The Legend of Zelda: Ocarina of Time* for the Nintendo 64 console. When players meet Princess Zelda for the first time, they can glance up at Hyrule Castle. Inside the window are three small posters of Mario, Bowser, and Luigi.

In the Mario game *Super Mario RPG: Legend of the Seven Stars*, gamers can glimpse sprites of both Link and Samus Aran.

Link from *Legend of Zelda*

EPIC BATTLES

The strategy behind choosing a weapon. The "pow!" of getting the perfect hit. The bright lights of an explosion. For decades, gamers have picked up their controllers to plug in and battle. Fighting and first-person shooter games, such as, *Call of Duty*, *Halo*, and *Fortnite*, have become extremely popular. These games may seem straightforward, but they are full of secrets. And despite their serious themes, some of the stunts are downright silly.

GAME WITHIN A GAME

Did you know? *Call of Duty: Black Ops Cold War* includes a secret retro game! Unlock the secret door inside the safe house. There, you'll be able to access *ZORK*, a game from 1980.

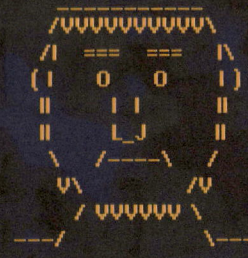

Mortal Kombat was released in 1992 by game company Midway.

One of today's top eSports franchises is *Counter-Strike*—but it didn't start as its own game. *Counter-Strike* was a **modification (mod)** for the game *Half-Life*. There are several other mods for *Half-Life*, but *Counter-Strike* is definitely the most well known.

What's another video game that secretly started as something else? *Halo*. *Halo* might be the most famous Xbox franchise of all time. There are *Halo* spin-off games, books, toys, and even a movie. It helped make Xbox popular. But the game almost wasn't released on Xbox. In fact, it was originally created for Apple. Microsoft swooped in and bought the game's **developer**. Remember that the next time you power up your Xbox for a game of *Halo*!

Xbox Series S Controller

MODIFICATION (mah-duh-fi-KAY-shuhn): a change by players or fans of a game that modifies one or more parts of a video game, such as visuals or game play

DEVELOPER (di-VEL-uhpur): a person or company who creates computer software, such as video games

Xbox Series X

You don't have to be an expert gamer to find Easter eggs in some of the top battle games. One of the creators of *Halo* actually hid himself within *Halo 2* and *Halo 3*. The hidden Easter egg is known as the "dancing half-naked man"!

Fans of *Fortnite* know that the game features some iconic Marvel heroes. The Season 4 map is scattered with Marvel-themed Easter eggs. Next time you play, look out for Tony Stark's workshop and the law offices of Jennifer Walters (She-Hulk). Keep your eyes on the screen, and you'll see that famous fighting games are full of countless Easter eggs.

Halo
Master Chief

NEW GAME, OLD SECRETS

In the 2020 game *Cyberpunk 2077*, players can complete a mission that will lead them to an extra-special Easter egg. It's a figurine from a classic fighting game—*Mortal Kombat*!

RULES OF THE GAME

Some of the most popular eSports out there are actually, well, sports! *NBA 2K*, *Madden NFL*, and *FIFA* are championship franchises. But even sports-themed video games break the rules every once in a while. Some major secrets are hiding in your favorite sports video games.

To start, there's *Wii Sports*. Released in 2006 for the Nintendo Wii, it's still one of the best-selling games of all time. Inside, players can find countless Easter eggs. Some of the sneaky features: Changing your bowling ball color, making the crowd laugh, and wearing silver boxing gloves.

Some Easter eggs are a little bit rotten. For years, games like *NCAA Football* and *NCAA March Madness* have given gamers the chance to play as their favorite college sports stars. But did you know that those players didn't make any money from the games? As college athletes, they were forbidden from earning money with their likenesses.

Luckily, this is starting to change. In 2020, EA Sports settled a lawsuit with the student-athletes featured in their games. As part of the settlement, $60 million will be paid to over 24,000 athletes. However, the NCAA hasn't yet decided if future student-athletes will be able to make money for their likenesses in games.

HUNTING DOWN A WIN

Madden NFL is one of the longest-running franchises. The team at Madden knows Easter eggs well. In fact, over the past few years, the game has run Easter egg hunt events. When gamers logged in each day, they could find coins, collectibles, players, and more.

Some video games aren't about sports. They are sports! Well, sort of. **Exergames** combine gaming with exercise. One of the first was Nintendo's *World Class Track Meet*. The 1986 game was all about running. In the early to mid-2000s, games like *Wii Fit* and *Xbox Fitness* got gamers moving.

Ring Fit Adventure is a Nintendo Switch exergame that combines a role-playing game with exercise. Even exergames have Easter eggs (or should we say exer-eggs?). *Ring Fit Adventure* has a secret rhythm game in its start menu.

> **EXERGAMES** (EK-sur-games): fitness games, or games that are also a form of exercise

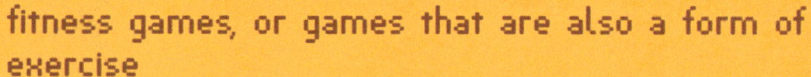

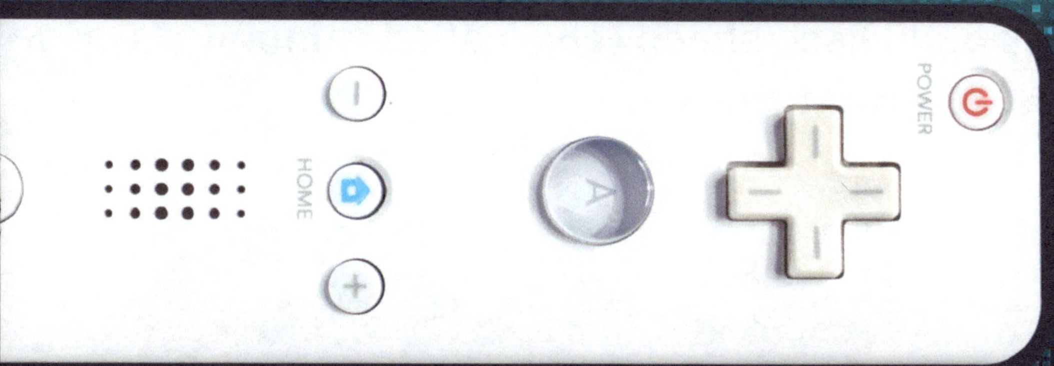

IN THE SANDBOX

Not all video games are about beating high scores, crushing enemies, and becoming a champion. Some of today's most unique games are about creativity. Simulation games let players recreate the real world. *SimCity*, *The Sims*, and *Stardew Valley* are famous simulation games.

For even more freedom, players can dive into **sandbox** games. These offer the ultimate in creativity. Have you played *Minecraft*? It's one of the most successful sandbox games of all time—and it's *full* of Easter eggs. Pirate Speak and Disco sheep (also called rainbow sheep) are two favorites.

SANDBOX (SAND-bahks): a video game type that gives players much or total creativity in how they play, sometimes without any formal goals or rewards

APRIL FOOLS'

Minecraft players look forward to April 1st every year. On April Fools' Day, joke features and updates are released. Some of them, like stained glass, eventually show up in the official game!

The *Animal Crossing* franchise is a sandbox full of secrets. There are lots of **crossovers** between Nintendo games and *Animal Crossing: New Horizons (ACNH)*. Throughout the game, there are references to *Splatoon 2*, *StarTropics*, and *The Legend of Zelda*. In 2021, a major crossover celebrated the 35th anniversary of *Super Mario Bros*. For the first time, players could access Mario-themed furniture while playing *ACNH*. Why choose just one video game when you can (sort of) play two?

CROSSOVERS (KRAWS-oh-vurs): games, levels, or fictional situations where two or more characters from different franchises are featured in the same game

For spooky secrets, look no further than *Grand Theft Auto (GTA)*. This franchise is known for its mashup of an open world with mission-driven gameplay. And of course, it's full of Easter eggs. Ghosts, UFOs, aliens, and even Bigfoot can be spotted throughout *GTA V*. The games are also packed with references to other games, movies, TV shows, books, and more. It pays to pay attention when you play *GTA*.

So, are you ready to level up and unlock the secrets hidden within your favorite games? If you watch closely and practice your gameplay, you'll be sure to spot some surprises. Discovering Easter eggs is one surefire way to prove that you're an eSports expert, a champion of the controller . . . a *gamer*, through and through.

THE SIMS SECRET

The characters in *The Sims* games speak a language called Simlish. Created by Will Wright, the language is made up of gibberish speech. But it doesn't just exist in *The Sims*. In fact, it first debuted in 1996's *SimCopter*. And civilized creatures in *Spore* can be taught to speak Simlish!

MEMORY GAME

Look at the pictures. What do you remember reading on the pages where each image appeared?

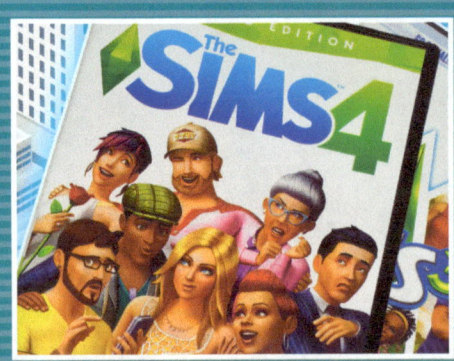

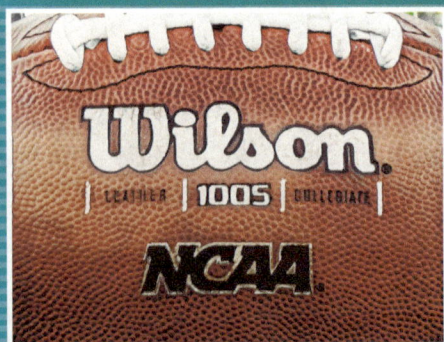

INDEX

console(s) 5, 6, 10
controller(s) 8, 12, 14, 28
Easter egg (s) 4, 6, 8, 10, 16, 18, 20, 21, 22, 24, 28
exercise 22, 23
fighting game(s) 12, 16
first-person shooter 10, 12, 22, 26

Mario 7, 10, 26
Nintendo 10, 18
secret(s) 4, 6, 7, 8, 12, 17, 18, 22, 26, 28, 29
simulation 24
sports 18, 20, 22
xBox 14, 22

AFTER-READING QUESTIONS

1. What are three examples of video game Easter eggs?
2. Why do you think Easter eggs are included in video games?
3. Why are video game secrets called "Easter eggs"?
4. Do you think student-athletes should get paid for appearing in video games?
5. What are two popular types or genres of video games?

ACTIVITY

It's your turn to be the video game developer. Think about your favorite game. If you were developing it, what Easter egg would you add? Maybe it would be a picture of yourself, a funny song, a cheat code, or a character from another game. The choice is yours! Draw a picture of the Easter egg and include a short paragraph explaining how gamers would find it. Don't make it too easy to find. The hunt is part of the fun!

ABOUT THE AUTHOR

Kaitlyn Duling is a lifelong lover of video games. She enjoys games that get her moving, thinking, and dreaming. When she's not on her Nintendo Switch, Kaitlyn is writing and living in Washington, DC. She has authored over 100 books for kids and teens.

© 2022 Rourke Educational Media

All rights reserved. No part of this book may be reproduced or utilized in any form or by any means, electronic or mechanical including photocopying, recording, or by any information storage and retrieval system without permission in writing from the publisher.

www.rourkeeducationalmedia.com

PHOTO CREDITS ©: page 01: amtitus/Getty Images; page 4: carloscastilla/ Getty Images; page 5: kasezo/ Getty Images; page 7: marysuperstudio/ Shutterstock.com; page 7: CharacterFamily/ Shutterstock.com; page 7: sansak/ Getty Images; page 7: Mile Atanasov/ Shutterstock.com; page 8: vectorsws/ Shutterstock.com; page 9: Peter Gudella/ Shutterstock.com; page 9: Lukmanazis/ Shutterstock.com; page 11: camilkuo/ Shutterstock.com; page 11: Stanislav Kogiku/ZUMAPRESS/Newscom; page 11: FUN FUN PHOTO/ Shutterstock.com; page 12: NEW LINE CINEMA / Album/ Newscom; page 13: Stasia04/ Shutterstock.com; page 13: Ahmad Arianto/Shutterstock.com; page 14: Miguel Lagoa/ Shutterstock.com; page 15: Stockcrafterpro/ Shutterstock.com; page 17: oseph Creamer/ Shutterstock.com; page 19: REDPIXEL.PL/ Shutterstock.com; page 19: burakguler/ Shutterstock.com; page 21: LUCAS JACKSON/REUTERS/Newscom; page 21: imging/ Shutterstock.com; page 21: Zach Chew/ Shutterstock.com; page 23: MARIO ANZUONI/REUTERS/Newscom; page 23: seeshooteatrepeat/ Shutterstock.com; page 25: Ismail Rajo/ Shutterstock.com; page 25: Oleksii Synelnykov/ Shutterstock.com; page 27: Leonel Calara/ Shutterstock.com; page 27: Barone Firenze/ Shutterstock.com; page 29: dean bertoncelj/ Shutterstock.com; page 29: Alexzel/ Shutterstock.com

Edited by: Jennifer Doyle
Cover design and illustration by: Joshua Janes
Interior design and illustrations by: Joshua Janes

Library of Congress PCN Data

Level Up Secrets Of The Games We Love / Kaitlyn Duling
 (Gaming and eSports)
 ISBN 978-1-73164-933-1 (hard cover)
 ISBN 978-1-73164-881-5 (soft cover)
 ISBN 978-1-73164-985-0 (e-Book)
 ISBN 978-1-73165-037-5 (e-Pub)
Library of Congress Control Number: 2021935548

Rourke Educational Media
Printed in the United States of America
04-1362413053